To Whom It Must Concern

To Whom It Must Concern

Poems

by
Claire van Breemen Downes

North Star Press of St. Cloud, Inc.

Library of Congress Cataloging-in-Publication Data

Downes, Claire van Breemen, 1926-
    To whom it must concern : poems / by Claire van Breemen
        Downes.—1st. ed.
        p. cm.
        ISBN 0-87839-185-1 (pbk. : alk. paper)
        I. Title.

PS3604.06898 T6 2002
811'.6--dc21
                                                                                  2002069591

Copyright © 2002 Claire van Breemen Downes

ISBN: 0-87839-185-1

First Edition

Printed in the United States of America
by Versa Press, Inc., East Peoria, Illinois

Published by
North Star Press of St. Cloud, Inc.
P.O. Box 451
St. Cloud, Minnesota 56302

Dedicated
to
Alan

Bright as a fire that haunts the night,
braving with flame my sky-dark grief,
you came
and flooded my chilled quietness
with warmth and noise and splendor past belief.

Table of Contents

Auditions for *Our Town*   1
Wedding Psalm   2
Marriage   3
Another Fairy Tale   4
Old Newspaper   7
After the Night Shift   8
Sammamish Summer   9
Birthday Tree   11
How Brief the Edens   12
Quiet Morning   14
Pendleton   15
Tupelo Tree and Tristan   18
Paw-paw and Persimmon   19
Wife   20
Not Writing of Love Making   21
Round the Block   22
Under Fire   23
Yesterday's Place   24
Drowning Creek   25
Impotence   26
Kentucky April   27
Role   28
Anonymous Casualty   29
Twenty Years from North Dakota   31

The Captive on a Very Bad Day   32
The Choice   34
Perfect Nightmare   35
Late Anniversary   36
An Uncompleted Work   37
Golden Time   38
In Absentia   39
Postcard to Lancelot   40
Island of White Birds   41
First Walk in Spring   42
Pile of Papers   43
Cocoons and Parents   44
Maple Leaf   46
Long Marriage   47
Lake Woods, October   48
Bagatelle   49
Fortieth Class Reunion   50
Motel Mirror   51
The Gold Watch   52
Across the Table   53
Sometime Visitor   55
Careless Persephones   56
Unauthorized Version   57
After Forty-five Years   58
Woven Life   59
Words Fail Me   60
Eternal Token   61
Love Song at Evening   64
Acknowledgments   67

AUDITIONS FOR *OUR TOWN*

The hall was empty. Then you came
        and wrote your name
        within the book.
        You stayed and took
my spacious afternoon away.
        We read the play.
        We tried the parts.
        We lost our hearts.
An endless minute waltz began
        within that span—
        our pas de deux,
        just me with you.

WEDDING PSALM

On this brave day,
turn to each other
as you have turned
and chosen. Here is your hoard
of strength and hope and laughter,
your salve for wounds,
your fate and food forever.
Take,
       give
              and be renewed.

MARRIAGE

You carry in your side   unknowing
        a cave-ly place   Adam's essential wound.
Battered by too much world
        I grow down very small
              curl me there hidden
emerge full-grown again and whole.

For you
        I think I am a tree.
You come
        beset   pursued   gasping
lean against me.
        My branches close about you
              and you rest.

ANOTHER FAIRY TALE

But you, my darling, should have married the prince. . . .
                                        Anne Sexton

I did marry the prince, love—
        the prince with raven hair   one lock
                falling with devastating innocence
                over his forehead,
        the prince   whose dark-amber eyes devoured me,
                who danced with me beneath magnolias
                        kissing my eyebrow.
        And I clung to his lean youngness, as he to me.
We were what we had always wanted   had waded
        swamps   walked blistering sands   to find.
The perfumed moons of the magnolias
        smiled down through a tangle of caught stars
and we danced on.

I married the prince   and we lived happily ever after—
        army-cots lashed together for a bridal bed
     barracks apartments   curb-yellow floors
          scrap-lumber furniture with cinder-blocks
     Proust and bean-soup and Jane Austen and the Turner Thesis
          the typewriter clicking   arias rising
          the diaper-pail boiling on the hotplate.

The prince was in search of his kingdom.
     The old car   bubbling with children
          careened on to the new maybe
               and the next.
     Our singing rippled across the country like tears.

We lived happily ever after   walked unaware
          through the minefield   paled only later
     clinging to each other   at the lurid bursts rising—
          detonations we had missed.

                    "They lived happily ever after,"
                    Grandma used to say
                    putting down the story-book
                    tucking the covers around our necks
                    "until they came to a tin bridge.
                         Tin bridge bended
                         and now my story is ended."
                    Kissing us, turned out the light.

Happy ever after.   Our small ones march
      to their own maybes. We are come
            to the valley of tin bridges.   They lurk
treacherous   spanning every stream.

      Tin bridges bend.
      Stories end.
I did marry the prince.

OLD NEWSPAPER

Remember? I shook with crying.
You had a dreadful time hushing me.
Even loving was not really enough.

      It was the picture laughing. . .
      the picture bride and groom. . .
      five years. . . the bride murdered. . .
      the picture still laughing. . .
      the picture hideously laughing
      under the grim caption.

And I would not be quiet
    until you promised to hide
    all laughing pictures.
    To hide? To destroy?
    Promised what? I do not know.
Yet now I understand:
    such sharp grief
    was not for a stranger.

AFTER THE NIGHT SHIFT
(Graduate School Mornings)

Breakfast was late those days.
Shushed by an early round
of orange juice, Cheerios,
small ones played softly.
Morning tiptoed in.

Just early enough
I started the coffee.
Heated the pan
for scrambled eggs.
Loaded the toaster.
When the hour hand
reached nine
I put the needle in the groove
of our Beethoven trio—
your chosen alarm.

Stumbling from sleep
you kissed me.
Day began.

SAMMAMISH SUMMER

Last night, not yet sleeping,
    I was in our house again,
        stepping out onto the slate doorstep,
            into the grass, cool-damp.
Morning edits the night, speaking of change:
    My garden is sodded over now.
        Its small irregular strip flows,
      indistinguishably green,
          beneath the birch.
Yet always, in my dreams,
    pansies, nasturtiums,
        press cool against my feet.

Down by the river where we swam,
    the tall catalpas lit huge pale candles
        in late pink evenings.
    I close my mind
    to dredged and deepened channel,
      straightened shore,
        our tall trees vanished.

For me this river rushes only backward.
    Under the trees,   the children's cove
    still there.   The small busy ones,
    still baking mud pies on its careful barricade,
        do not hear me.
        Her mink-brown hair,
        his dandelion-fluff
  bend together   intent.
I reach to hold those lost and perfect ones again,
    but they do not come when I call. All disappears:
        that green golden summer
        that last best summer. . . .

Why is there sadness in remembering happy times
        even in happy times?

BIRTHDAY TREE
(sijo)

The split-leaf birch you planted on our river-bottom acre
Took root and flourished, perhaps to prove the skeptic grumblers wrong
Reached green maturity. We were the ones uprooted and dislodged.

HOW BRIEF THE EDENS
(Pantoum)

How brief the Edens we are given to hold—
How swiftly slip the days we long to keep!
Still, memory holds beauty, frozen-gold,
And dreams bring back lost laughter to our sleep.

We gather up our treasure in a heap,
Thinking to cling to all that we enfold.
We never guess, until our time to weep,
How brief the Edens we are given to hold.

Time seems stuck fast—an old, dull whale fast-shoaled.
We rest contented; honeyed hours creep—
We cannot understand, though we are told,
How swiftly slip the days we long to keep.

That drab leviathan with one tail's sweep
Can crush the walls that keep us from the cold,
Shatter our happiness—but, buried deep,
Still memory holds beauty, frozen-gold.

Its glint can spark new fires, if we are bold,
To warm us. While we watch the fresh flames leap,
Today and yesterday in one are rolled,
And dreams bring back lost laughter to our sleep.

Beyond the garden's gate, the path grows steep.
Thorns tear at us; the grackles swoop and scold.
We reach the outer world. We sow and reap,
And dread the winter's coming, and grow old.
                              How brief the Edens!

QUIET MORNING

I crouch in an eggshell of time.
Its fragile arc
      suspends the crushing lumber of the day
      bears all weights.

                    Round white peace,
you have only a moment.
      The passion is for omelets.

PENDLETON

A place-name falls. In a car speeding to the airport,
three people step into dry rivers of remembering:

The Husband	That summer I finished my degree. . .
	Waiting to hear of a college job for fall,
	I worked at public relations
	for the power company—
	driving all over the hot, dusty city,
	talking to people with huge bills
	to show them someone cared.
	No relief I could offer, actually,
	though some scribbled reports
	may have brought action.
	Mostly folks told me why themselves—
	the fluctuations, the sharp peaks of use.
	The sculptor-potter knew
	why her bill was high
	and laughed. But her kiln didn't
	get fired up too often now. The children
	played about the kitchen floor. Later, she said.
	I thought of my own wife,
	her arrested momentum,
	the children, the wretched house—

lucky enough to find even that—
this whole suspended summer.
Waiting for life to begin.

The Wife	Heat. Dust. The venomous landlady hated children, hated *college* (mouthing the dirty word) women like me. Mostly she just hated. Never spoke softly to me, to any of us, from the time her caretaker rented me that shack on the back of the lot. She scolded the old man well. Afraid of being sued for damages, I suppose, or fined for housing code violations. We had come by in an early evening, freed from the rented room that held our days. Nearly a week I had watched the papers for a house, an apartment, housekeeping rooms. There were none. So each day when the killing blaze of the sun eased, I propped the tiny one carefully in the stroller, took the toddler by the hand, called the others, and the five of us set forth in solemn cavalcade, looking for empty houses, signs on lawns, any hope of shelter— The shack was what we found. I worried about fire with the children asleep in that tiny loft. No tub to bathe them.

They danced through the sprinkler
hot afternoons. I remember
the filthy sewage rising in the shower
when the plumbing failed.
Afraid, always tired—
lucky the college job came through
before the eviction notice.
      But why can't I recall the shape of our days?
      I can't even remember the baby's crying.

The Passenger, Who Grew Up There

Summer then was long as a year
    and splendid as the sun. Hot, yes. Always hot.
Afternoons we kids swam
      the irrigation ditches, sometimes the pool.
Riding and picnics.
    In fall, the rodeo:
slim-hipped cowboys   crowds of tourists
      a swirl of parties.
        The spring I graduated,
      parties were perpetual. It was such fun.
You'd think no one had ever graduated
      before; no one had ever been young;
      it had never, ever been spring before.
Only then. Only for us.

      This talk of gritty dust—
    I only remember a golden haze
      sifting down summer streets.

TUPELO TREE AND TRISTAN

On some far, half-remembered day
When sudden rain drew silver castle walls
Tight-curtained round us,
We sipped the beaded magic of the cup—
Sweet fire upon the tongue.

We drank, yet lived.
Now, all these mornings after
The honey-potion flavors yet our days—
A sorcerer's brew within the coffee-cups,
A heady sweetness in the marmalade.

PAW-PAW AND PERSIMMON

I thrust my hand
      among the still-unleafed branches
          of the persimmon;

Pluck the orange moon, swollen-ripe;

Devour,
      letting the juice run
          to my elbows.

Puzzled, the children come
      to tell me,
   "There is no moon."

I answer softly,
         "Last night the persimmon bore fruit,
   though the paw-paw has only silly brown blossoms."

WIFE

I am your clothesline.
    All your fresh-laundered theories
        flap publicly in the sun.
    Well-aired and neatly folded
        I bring them in at night.

I am your waste-basket.
    Discarded rages clutter me—
        small, broken weapons
            meant for someone else.

Yet I am your piano
    for the trying out of tunes
        with no one else to hear.

NOT WRITING OF LOVE-MAKING

    once I looked deep into
    the pearlescent back feathers
    of a swan   I've never
       found words for that
            either.

ROUND THE BLOCK

We walk together in our evening street.
Venus hangs low and golden in the west.
Though we speak only, softly, of the heat,
Our touches tell us that we know we're blest.
The sounds of summer murmur in the dark:
A mother calls a child who lingers late;
Hunched adolescents gabble near the park;
Across the background grumbles a slow freight.
Roses and phlox are heavy in the air—
Alyssum, too, now we are nearly back.
You clutch me, fearful I will stumble where
The lawn beneath our trees yawns ink-blot black.

Reaching our door-yard ends a little part
Of this long journey we walk heart-in-heart.

UNDER FIRE

Marriage
is the wall
we put our backs to
side by side
repel attackers
foil the vengeful.
Our strength
behind us
sheltering and sure.

YESTERDAY'S PLACE

Small dreams return to touch the vanished land,
      to trace the bear-slumped mountain we have loved,
          its shapes and shadows changing in the sun,
      to snatch at manzanita and madrone,
          or test the snow-cold of the noisy creek—
we climb to clear air,
          clouds about our feet.

Those days are gone.
      All mountains out of reach.
The present is forever.
That's enough.

DROWNING CREEK

Drowning Creek
is the border of Madison County.
We should have known. Someone
should have told us. It might
have made a difference.

Flat   innocent
across its sand   its stone
the shallow water barely moves.
Drowning?   Once maybe
spring floods
other years   other centuries.
Drowning there now   would be
an act of will   pushing one's face
into a pool of sky   fracturing
the bough-crossed blue
breaking the mold of living.

In Madison County   breaking molds
is always an act of will
always a drowning.

IMPOTENCE

The dogs must die, of course.
They found the sow and her litter,
stole four suckling pigs before being caught.
(We should have thrashed them when they killed the possum.
We should have punished them for chasing rabbits.
We should have kept them chained—)

    The farmer kindly cruel, "We can't have that—"
    Of course not. Who could argue?

The dog-warden is half-deaf and seldom used.
In this country of hunters
men do their own killing.
    We are outlanders. Gunless. Weak.
    For us he will come.
    Sometime.

Sometime is slow.
Penned, our once-joyous dogs wail, going mad.
    Stomach-knotted, shamed,
        I muse on the swift mercy
        of a loaded gun
        and a sure hand.

KENTUCKY APRIL

Let spring happen.
Let us watch
in unashamed tranquillity.

Not for us again
shall these trees thrust forth lilacs,
the small, bright buds of japonica
wall in the steep lane,
nor the solitary tulip flame and fall.

The forsythia picked for yesterday's table
is golden against next year's dark,
and the violets spilled purple on the lawn
must be cherished against our coming cold.

Cling to all these as to each other.
Out of many promises
we have nothing else.

ROLE

I hang in festoons
on a family tree;
Festoons of what you will—
strung cranberries,
nourishing bits of suet,
small twinkling lights—
Changing to what is needed. Trying
not to be popcorn
when the demand is tinsel
nor twinkling lights
when small birds starve.

ANONYMOUS CASUALTY

Lost somewhere
      in a welter of bluebirds and cub scouts
          civic duty   whir of vacuum cleaner
Dear Senator   Please consider
     several amendments to your welfare plan
purr of the sewing machine   p.t.a. needs your support
     if payment has been made in past ten days
          please disregard
      washer spins telephone rings
    our regular meeting has been rescheduled
        vote yes   save our city
Please, Senator   the dignity of human beings
    request pleasure of your company
        is your family protected
amazing special offer   what's for dessert   Mama

     somewhere
        behind lists and schedules
   Senator   plead for the right of a person to choose the task
         are *you* recycling cans
parents of scholarship applicants must fill out these forms
        remember to buy dog-food
     Senator   the right to choose one's task

Lost somewhere.

The victim as yet is unidentified.

All identifying marks had been removed.

TWENTY YEARS FROM NORTH DAKOTA

I dreamed I could not return to Minot.
I had thought to go   finish everything necessary
    be back in time for an early dinner.
But the pavement was cracked and broken.
The bleached-gold grasses stood
      tall and ragged   in the crevices.

Standing there where the road turned off,
    the child heavy upon my arm
        quiet despite his illness
        (what child, I do not know—only that he was mine
          and he was ill)
I looked up the crazed concrete trail
    feeling night coming on
        and my own weariness.

My dream provided a small village there.
In the shelter of the old store
    my urgency all anxiously forgot
I phoned you:"Come. Take me home."
        It was the only thing to do.

THE CAPTIVE ON A VERY BAD DAY

I never said it was not honorable:
    tidying the cups and spoons
    cleaning the hair-soap slime from the bathroom sink drains
    remembering to wash the greasy filter from the kitchen fan
    strolling the noisy vacuum   not forgetting to look for
        cobwebs on the ceiling
    keeping the counter glaring-clean
    demolishing the day's accumulated clutter
        swift   certain   ruthless   no hesi-
        tation over   anonymous grimy
        treasures.

Honorable.   Necessary.   Achievable.
    Easy, in fact.   Some women
put the last shiningness in place
    by 10 a.m.   trot next door
    for coffee   in their curlers
    and a good gossip   talk to their TV
all afternoon   wondering why there isn't
    something more.

Bewildered   still alien after twenty years
         I search for order   unrequited.
Not joy of bread rising   nor fragrance
of well-seasoned food   not even
small clasping arms   nor all
delirious crumbs of gladness
can compensate.   I am a stranger
wandering.   I dress in someone else's clothes,
struggle unskilled   with someone else's task
consuming me.   Over there
my own work lies waiting.

But housewifery is honorable.
Always honorable.

THE CHOICE

"A simple matter of priorities,"
you say.
"Decide what you want—
writing poetry
or a clean house."

Dear heart,
I have always known
what I wanted!
To write poetry
in a clean house.

PERFECT NIGHTMARE

I slammed the door on my untidy world
grumpily slept.
Dream-woke a Sabbath
Eden-pure.
Sun-summoned   staggered grumbling to my chores.

Chores?   Iridescent order rippled over all.
The gleaming kitchen tile laughed in my face.
My children   scrubbed and comfortably fed
sat easily in unaccustomed robes—
decorum   amity   fraternal love.
Laundry, then,   I mumbled   groping on   still unaware.
No!   *Even the ironing!*

The garden?
Weeded rows stretched green perfection.
Attic?   Basement?
Parlor-clean.
Grateful   uneasy   sank down at my desk
Unwieldy gift of time to write a poem!
But all the poems were written.

LATE ANNIVERSARY

Just this remains of what you loved and sought:
    The taut-skinned bone where once the soft cheek curved;
    The deep-pressed path where our sweet laughter ran;
    The blue-washed hollows that have held my tears.
Yet all lost beauty—mirrored in you—lives,
wraps me more richly than the robe of youth.

    Wherefore my eyes light candles to your name;
    my dove hands flutter to make sacrifice.

AN UNCOMPLETED WORK

From the days of half our lives
we have woven a careful table-covering
on which to spread
our sturdy bread and wine
our pebble treasures.
So neat a work would not be cleanly unraveled
would rend distorted
fibers tearing   reaching out
seeking their other selves.
Only the ultimate scissors
can divide this tidily.
Meanwhile
our fingers stumble
groping towards each other
still busily weaving.
We understand the pattern now
remember the intricate meaning of
each thread   why
bright gold runs here   and silver here
and where the dark threads are.

Admiring friends think the work complete
find us still at the loom
weaving-in another day.

GOLDEN TIME
(Pantoum)

In this sweet, radiant summer of our life,
      The honey oozes golden from the comb.
The grain that greened so early now is ripe.
      Honey and harvest we bear gladly home.

The honey oozes golden from the comb,
      Amber to liven all our winter bread.
Honey and harvest we bear gladly home—
      Our sunlight for the graying months ahead,

Amber to liven all our winter bread.
      Shared fragrance nourishes our daily song,
Our sunlight for the graying months ahead,
      Brightness and comfort, though the dark seems long.

Shared fragrance nourishes our daily song
      In this sweet, radiant summer of our life.
Brightness and comfort. Though the dark seems long,
      The grain that greened so early now is ripe.

IN ABSENTIA

My fingers remember your bones:
    the hollows of your shoulder-blades,
    the craggy stepstones of your vertebrae,
    the changing textures of your skin.

My fingers remember your bones,
    as loss recalls loved landscapes,
    far from home.

POSTCARD TO LANCELOT

Castle is cold without you.
Bring me daffodils
      to warm the rain.

ISLAND OF WHITE BIRDS

Remember the island of white birds?
      Remember?
Manatee mangroves, a white flower blooming—
      Remember?
Blooming as day fades,
          the petals come winging.
     Remember the island of white birds.

Remember the island of white birds,
     the herons homing at sunset.
         Remember?
     Thirty-three years we have watched
     the flower that blooms in the twilight.

The mangroves tire of their burden.
We circle home with the herons.
     Remember the island of white birds.

FIRST WALK IN SPRING
(Lachesis)

Though grimy snow lies thick, sunlight is gaining.
Gurgling down gutter pipes, winter is draining.
Dry pavements have only puddles remaining.

Melt all the dregs and lees! Off with the season!
We want the tyrant gone, and we have reason.

All the long bitter weeks winter was gripping,
ice covered all our ways. Endlessly slipping,
we learned to stay within. Now winter's dripping.

Triumph in his disgrace! Off with the season!
Now, as he moves offstage, we gain our reason.

Cabined, we found ourselves fretful and ailing,
mopish with fancied ills, and our skin paling.
Now see the tables turned: winter is failing.

Speed winter on his way! Off with the season!
We'll cheer to see him go, and we have reason.

Now we are free at last from winter's tether.
Now we return again to open weather.
Once more we're side by side, walking together.

PILE OF PAPERS

I could write a poem
      of a man and a woman
squabbling over a clutter of correspondence
      on the dining-table. As they grow
older, smaller   the pile
      mounds higher. They burrow into it
at last.   As they turn
      into scuttling spiders
the woman wins   of course.

COCOONS AND PARENTS
(Rondeau Redoublé)

Now that time comes we sing no lullaby.
This pillow holds no more the sleep-swirled head.
No infant wakes us with a midnight cry—
That portion of our parenthood is fled.

I think of bedtime stories I have read—
Frogs, princelings, beanstalks, elephants-that-fly.
I look back, wistful, at the sweet hours sped,
Now that time comes we sing no lullaby.

I catch my breath and turn back, with a sigh—
No use to look more at the empty bed!
Those small ones walk the world and ride the sky;
This pillow holds no more the sleep-swirled head.

Forgotten are the childish tears they shed,
Forgotten the hot words and tempers high.
Silences flood the house where noise once spread.
No infant wakes us with a midnight cry.

Once the word patterning our days was "Why?"
Once song and study leavened all our bread.
Time was we served up fractions with the pie—
That portion of our parenthood is fled.

We always knew and wise ones always said
No lullabies are needed by and by—
Cocoons and parents: fated to be shed.
There are new melodies that we must try,
Now that time comes.

MAPLE LEAF

From pale-green spring
to summer emerald
I wave serenely.
Spread generously
to shelter those oppressed
by summer sun.
When autumn comes
my nurturing days
are over.
Now is the time
to flame
before I fall.

LONG MARRIAGE

In the tangle of love
arms and legs
are reassembled,
hard to sort out.
Hair twines.
Breaths fuse.
Visceral murmurings
seem mutual.
One flesh.

In the tangle of years
yours / mine
blur,
no longer matter.
Family myths
merge, multiply.
Thoughts
need no words.
One.

LAKE WOODS, OCTOBER

I saw a white birch
    like a harp unstrung.
Where should I search
    for all its songs unsung?

BAGATELLE

Golden lads when I was young
      danced my heart away—
spoke my name with honeyed tongue
      and called me out to play.

One came later to the ball,
      drew me to his side,
never went away at all
      and would not be denied.
So we danced our life as one,
      waltz and minuet.
Though too soon the dance is done,
      its music echoes yet.

FORTIETH CLASS REUNION

"Make the world go away,"
the music crooned as we danced.
Close together. Dreamy-eyed.
Couples swaying as one body.
Chaperones would have cluck-clucked
in those old days we tried now to relive.
But our chaperones had gone long since,
leaving us on our own
and still not sure.

"Make the world go away!"
the tune insisted. And we,
struggling to keep the world
within our grasp,
liking it rather well
and lacking some sure alternative,
danced on and on,
trying to pretend that earth
was not really slipping
from under our feet

while the music
made the world go away.

MOTEL MIRROR
(Variation on a Vanitas theme)

Shower mist erases
slowly as morning fog
lifts soft from tree-top-pebbled hills.
Dim-rising into light
the mountain nymph appears.
Lithe as yesterday.
Luminous with youth.

The squab-built crone
stares back in disbelief.

THE GOLD WATCH

We speak of Florida.
Sudden visions: the packing   the partings
    the piano to sell   the antique chairs
    might bring a pretty sum   those
    saké cups (solemn small ones
    choosing Papa's birthday gift)   will they
    fit   some tiny alien house,
    that almost forgotten land
where we were young?

I walked the beach then
    estranged   hoarding unhappiness
    as though it were a rare seashell.
    My hair whipped across my face,
    my fists punched deep into pockets
    of the swaggering sailcloth jacket.
To recapture that sullen joy
could be worth upheaval.

We have confused time with geography.
This heavy sailcloth crumbles at my touch.

ACROSS THE TABLE

You sit unquiet—
      as you always have,
      in motion even when at rest,
burning the flesh from your bones.

Our blended years show in your face,
      colors and textures changed.
No luminous boy-child now.

White touches the bold eyebrows,
      shapes the beard you grew
      when you turned fifty.

I cannot see from here the silver filaments
      webbing the black hair, which even yet
          falls negligent across your brow.

(Close, on the pillow beside me,
      those gray hairs glint in the lamplight.
      To strangers, they are still
          almost a secret.)

I speak. You do not hear.
  (An old war, that one. We no longer keep score.)

Dragon-wrestling?
Castle-building?
What far mountain do you climb?

Now you glance down. Your glasses
      mirror your coffee cup.
Twin perfect circles, swirling, hide your eyes.

You look up, and you smile, eyes and all.
        You have returned to me.
                Always returned to me.

SOMETIME VISITOR

Rejoice that summer spends her day with us,
though she presumes upon our doting love
and overstays her welcome as a guest.
She dances rowdily with some old flame.
Her sun-kissed lips sing love-songs to the moon
She then feeds greedily at bounty's board
and sleeps inopportunely all asprawl
upon the parlor sofa, noisily—
her winning ways laid by for formal times.
She knows we shall forgive her presently
when she has spread her treasure round our feet
and bound its silver sheaves with her own hand.
Autumn knocks soon. They share a dance or two.
She flings a kiss, then hurries on her way.

We shall be long alone when winter comes.

CARELESS PERSEPHONES

The fruits of summer are gone.
We have rolled the globes of golden melon on our tongues,
      licked eagerly the dripping honey of the pear,
      gulped down the firm cleft peach,
           the grapes clotted with sun.

Devoured—
      and never reckoned up
           the total of our pomegranate seeds.

UNAUTHORIZED VERSION

Shakespeare's *Quatuor Novissima*, 1994 Edition

You see the deepening autumn of my year,
in which once-hopeful green leaves fade and fall
from off the shivering, wind-tossed trees, now clear
of sheltered nests and birds that chirp and call.

Here see my day's grey evening settling down,
the western sky still tinged with dying red.
Night's darkness soon will blanket all around,
like Death himself, who puts us all to bed.

The flame that lights my being now burns low
and flickers on the coals of yesterday—
sometime to die of that which made it grow,
become no more than ashes borne away.

All this you see. Small wonder that you choose
to cherish closely all you soon must lose.

AFTER FORTY-FIVE YEARS

Summer. A moonlight dance
      beneath magnolia trees.
A stage-set for romance
      and love's small victories.

Marriage. The sweet small years
      of bibs and grocery lists.
One metaphor recurs—
      magnolias through the mists.

This I assert though every precept fails:
Magnolias are as real as diaper pails.

WOVEN LIFE

Tight-woven textures of our yesterdays
wrap us more warmly than the airy gauze
we spun of feather dreams and autumn haze
when we were young.

Then we thought life a waltz without a pause
and planned our fashionings to suit our dance.
We disregarded minor flecks and flaws
when we were young.

Although we left the fabric all to chance,
life put some sturdy fibers in the loom
among the rainbow threads of bright romance
when we were young.

Therefore, though drafts blow cold in winter's room,
snug in the radiant total of our days,
we bask in surer warmth than love's new bloom
when we were young.

WORDS FAIL ME

They used to come running.
Now they scurry away.
Scrabble down rabbit holes.
Scuttle behind rocks.

Whole sentences
lined up in battle array
waver suddenly like raw recruits.
Break and run

leaving me betrayed.
Captive to an ancient enemy.

ETERNAL TOKEN

When my grave is broke up again. . .
    And he that digs it, spies
        A bracelet of bright hair about the bone.
                —John Donne, "The Relique"

Lovers all exchange some token
when they vow to love and cherish,
to keep faith until they perish,
long as firmaments endure—
should their vows remain unbroken,
all their bliss seems then secure.

Ah! but could we so secure
with a pledge and with a token
that our hearts would be unbroken,
then we might consent to cherish
one another and endure,
obdurate, until we perish.

Though the universe should perish,
we should keep our love secure.
Life it is that won't endure.
Truth to tell, this trifling token
will outlive the life you cherish.
This small bagatelle, unbroken,

will outlast the vow unbroken.
Things remain, but people perish.
Therefore, though you dare to cherish
one dear heart, and hold secure
life and love by one frail token,
just the bauble will endure.

So, love, since we can't endure
let our vows remain unbroken,
bound forever by this token.
Bracelets of bright hair don't perish—
bind the grave-bound bone secure,
leaving love to those we cherish.

Hear me, lovers, as you cherish
and—relinquishing—endure,
keep some circlet still secure,
symbol of your love unbroken—
sure that as your world shall perish,
your love lives within that token.

Love's true token which we cherish,

though we perish, shall endure
still unbroken, still secure.

LOVE SONG AT EVENING

Rest in the silver shadows a while,
Where leaves make lace of the sun's last rays,
Nor look to the road and the dust-gold haze
That covers tomorrow's urgent mile.

Rest in the silver shadows with me.
Forget that the day has blazed and died
In dusty triumph, small dreams denied.
Forget tomorrow.   Forgetting, see

We rest at last, love. Rest we must.
Others inherit the dream, the dust.

ACKNOWLEDGMENTS

The following poems have previously been published:

"Another Fairy Tale"	*The Moccasin*, 1993
"Cocoons and Parents"	*20 Poets Celebrate the Lake Country*, 1997
"Golden Time"	*33 Minnesota Poets*, Nodin Press, 2000
"Love Song at Evening"	*33 Minnesota Poets*
"Paw-paw and Persimmon"	*Nostoc Magazine* #17, Winter, 1988-1989
"Quiet Morning"	*The Moccasin*, 1994
"Round the Block"	*The Moccasin*, 1990

BIOGRAPHICAL NOTE

Claire van Breemen Downes, a native Midwesterner, met a transplanted New Englander while a graduate student at Florida State University. In the fifty years since, their teaching has taken them around the United States, as well as to Canada and Great Britain. She and her husband, Alan, returned at length to the Midwest and now live in St. Cloud, Minnesota, where she taught for many years in the English department of St. Cloud State University.

Her poetry has appeared in *The Great River Review, Tampa Review,* and other magazines, and in the Nodin Press collection, *33 Minnesota Poets,* in *Twenty Poets Celebrate the Lake District*, and in *Nine One One*, a nationwide anthology of commemorative poems. A short story, "Lena's Book," was published in an earlier Nodin volume, *26 Minnesota Writers*. In 1991, a story poem, "Marilla Melinda Melissa McClure," won the Loft Children's Literature Award for a picture-book manuscript, and the Society for the Study of Midwestern Literature recently announced that a selection from her unpublished novel, *They Labor in Vain,* has received their 2001 Paul Somers Award for Creative Prose. Some of her best creative works, her five children (and five grandchildren) must be counted as their own reward.

NORMANDALE COMMUNITY COLLEGE
LIBRARY
9700 FRANCE AVENUE SOUTH
BLOOMINGTON, MN 55431-4399